I Read
The News ⌐

A Play

Willy Russell

Samuel French – London
New York – Sydney – Toronto – Hollywood

Willy Russell is indebted to The Beatles for the title of this play, taken from their song of the same title.

I READ THE NEWS TODAY

First broadcast on BBC School Radio in the series "Listening and Writing" on 4th February, 1977

CHARACTERS

Ross, a local radio disc jockey
Voice (of a radio commercial)
Ronny (a youth on the run)
Police Constable
Police Sergeant
Newscaster
Interviewer

I READ THE NEWS TODAY

A local radio station

Ross, a disc jockey, is at the microphone

Ross OK. That's er . . . my Record of the Week. Don't think it'll be too long before that one's riding high in the national charts.

Music

And this is Paul Ross, with you until the crack of dawn. And tonight, I've got a deserted studio. Night Spin, tonight—it's just between ourselves . . . Let's cut out for a short break, before I bring you the news.

Voice (*on tape*) An orchestra? A band? A group? No. Just one man and one instrument can produce the sounds you hear. The SOUNDPACK! A revolution in music. With absolutely no knowledge of music. YOU can produce sounds like this.

Muzak

And this.

Muzak

SOUNDPACK is not just an instrument. It's a band at your fingertips. Have you ever wanted to produce great music, but not known how? Then SOUNDPACK is for you. SOUND-PACK—no knowledge of music required. SOUNDPACK— available at music shops, and most large department stores.

Muzak fades

Ross OK, Paul Ross back with you here on Night Spin. And it's time for the halfway news. (*He takes on a more formal news reader voice*) A dramatic escape in the city today. After being sentenced to eighteen months detention, a local youth made his escape from police who were leading him from the city's magistrates' court. The youth, Ronald Arthur Heron, made his

successful bid for freedom by jumping from a moving police van
after magistrates had convicted him of causing more than five
thousand pounds' worth of damage to goods in a local warehouse. In an act of what the magistrates called "mammoth,
unprovoked, mindless vandalism", Heron had single-handedly
smashed an entire floor of goods belonging to Pine Cash and
Carry Ltd. A police spokesman said that he expected Heron to
be apprehended "before very long". Local ratepayers met
council officials tonight in an effort to reduce rates in the city. A
spokesman . . . a spoke . . .

Ronny enters, brandishing a gun

There is a scuffle and the radio transmission is cut

Ronny Don't move! Right, just don't move, or y' dead. Right?

Ross Am I movin', man? Eh? Look, I mean . . . I'm not moving.
Don't shoot me. Please, whatever you want, you can have it.
Don't shoot me . . . please.

Ronny I won't shoot, if you don't move. I don't wanna hurt you,
so just be a good lad, an' do as y' told . . . Right . . . slowly . . .
move that chair back . . . Listen, mate . . . tell me the truth. Is
there any rope, tape, anythin' like that in here?

Ross (*terrified*) I don't know . . . man, I . . . I don't know . . .

Ronny What's up with you? Are y' gonna cry? I'm not gonna hurt
you. Are you worried about the gun? Well, just be a good lad,
an' I won't have to fire it. Come on, is there any rope in here?

Ross What for?

Ronny What for? What d'you think for? So we can play skippin'
games! I wanna tie you up, that's what for.

Ross There's . . . there's cable . . . you could use that.

Ronny Good thinkin', Batman.

Ross Look . . . there's some spare cable down there . . .

Ronny Get up slowly, an' pass it to me.

Ross I hope you . . . I hope you realize that when you cut the
transmission you probably alerted half the city that something
was wrong down here.

Ronny That's all right. Sit down there. As soon as I've got your
feet tied to this post, you'll be goin' back on an' tellin' them it
was just a technical hitch. Right? You just tell them it was a
fault, an' then stick an LP on. All right, put y' feet together.
Right, now tie them to that post.

Ross You've not gone to all this trouble just to get something played on the radio have you?

Ronny Don't try an' be smart, you.

Ross I'm sorry, man ... Look, I just ...

Ronny All right. Yeah. Maybe I am doin' all this just t' get something played on the radio. Not a record though. I couldn't care less about records. Just put anythin' on. But listen, mate. Do anythin' wrong an' you get this ... straight through the head. Right?

Ross Look, man ... I've told you ... I'll do just what you say, and nothing more ... honestly.

Ronny Right. I'll tell you what to say.

SCENE 2

A police station

Constable 'Ey, Sarge.

Sergeant What?

Constable I've just had about half a dozen calls sayin' the local radio station went off the air without any warnin'.

Sergeant Well, why are they ringin' us? Tell them to ring the radio station. Not the police station. We're coppers here. Not electricians. I don't know ...

Constable They said they can't get through. The telephone line's dead, as well.

Sergeant Wouldn't you think we had enough to cope with, eh? Get the transistor out the back. Let's have a listen.

SCENE 3

The radio studio

Ronny An' when you've told them that, I want you to put the record on. Then switch it so that it's only the record that's goin' out of here. I don't want them to hear us. Right?

Ross I'll do whatever you say ...

Ronny Good. 'Cos I don't wanna have to shoot you. OK. Go on.

Ross Paul Ross . . . er . . . here again with . . . er . . . apologies for
the loss of transmission. We've got the engineers in here trying
to sort out what went wrong, and . . . er . . . well, here's a record
while they try and sort out the problem.

SCENE 4

The police station

Sergeant What did I tell you? Put it off. I hate that rubbish.
Constable Sorry, Sarge, but we had to . . .

SCENE 5

The radio station

Ronny All right. OK, pal. Now just take it easy.

SCENE 6

The police station

Sergeant 'Ey! Hold on. Just switch that up.

SCENE 7

The radio studio

Ronny (*pointing to the panel of controls*) 'Ey! What's that switch?
It's still up.
Ross Which switch?
Ronny Which switch? That switch.
Ross Look man. You want the record transmitting. We can't
transmit anything without that.
Ronny Those microphones aren't on, are they?

Ross Of course not. Look, I'll speak into them. If they were live, you'd hear it amplified in the studio . . .

Ronny You just leave them alone. I'll try them, not you. Hello . . . hello . . . testin' one, two, three, testin' . . .

Ross I've told you man, they're dead. The only thing going out is the record.

Ronny Yeah . . . What's in that, that cubicle over there?

Ross That's the teleprinter. The news comes in on that.

Ronny I'm gonna have a look. Don't try anythin'. (*He goes to the cubicle*)

SCENE 8

The police station

Constable Shall I get a car round, Sarge?

Sergeant Eh? What for?

Constable Well you just heard it.

Sergeant What you talking about? It's just a play isn't it? That's all. Switch it off.

SCENE 9

The radio station

Ross (*speaking into the microphone*) A gun . . . he's got a . . . gun . . . he's got a . . .

The sound of paper rustling is heard from the cubicle

Ronny 'Ey . . . they're still lookin' for me.

Ross What?

Ronny Look, it's just come through on that typin' machine "Local police are still on the lookout for the youth who escaped outside the city magistrates' court today. The youth, Ronald Arthur Heron, had been convicted of causing more than five thousand pounds' worth of damage to goods belonging to Pine Cash and Carry Ltd."

Ross What! You mean that's you?

Ronny Course it is. An' this: listen. "Reports just coming in that the same warehouse was vandalized tonight. As yet no confirmation of a link between the two items."

Ross What? You escaped, then went back and did it again?

Ronny Yeah.

Ross Listen, man. Why hang around here, then? Why don't you split, now?

Ronny They'd only catch me, wouldn't they?

Ross But look, man, can't you see that you'll be caught if you hang around here?

Ronny You think I'm thick, don't you? Course I can see that. I'll get caught. I know that. But not till I've told them.

Ross Told who?

Ronny Them ... the people out there. The listeners. See, they never let anyone talk, y'know. Know that magistrate, that judge who did me today, eh? I tried to tell him, I did, you know. But he wouldn't listen. They never do, you know. I tried. I tried to tell him so's it'd get in the papers, an' that. No chance, though. He just started shoutin' an' abusin' me, didn't he. You know the form. "Mindless". "Vandal". "Unprovoked". "Senseless". You know, all that stuff. An' I was tryin' to tell him. There was no way he was gonna listen. No way. That's why I did a bunk. It's all lies, you know.

Ross What is?

Ronny All of it. It's all lies that they tell you. Like you. You're a liar!

Ross Listen, man ...

Ronny You are, you know. Like all the stuff you put out over the radio. It's all lies, isn't it? All lies an' cheatin' an' that. Rubbish it is.

Ross Look, I just play the records, and ...

Ronny I know what you do. I've listened to you. You even played a dedication for me once. *San Quentin* by Johnny Cash. D'you remember?

Ross Well ... er ... we get lots of requests for dedications ...

Ronny For me mam an' our Billy it was. Don't you remember?

Ross Yeah, yeah, I think I do ... yeah ... it's coming back, now.

Ronny Liar! You never remember anythin' like that. You don't give a thought for anyone who writes in to you. You just read out their dedications, an' then forget about them. You didn't even play *San Quentin*. You played *Boy Named Sue* instead.

Ross Look . . . I'm sorry, man.

Ronny It's all right. I hate Johnny Cash now, anyway. He's another liar. I used to think he was great. But he was all lies, as well. I found that out, you know. He was supposed to have been in prison an' on drugs an' all that. Supposed to be a hard man. He wasn't though. He didn't do any of that. He was just a singer. Lived all his life in a hotel in New York.

Ross Is that right?

Ronny Yeah. I've had enough of heroes now. Does the gun frighten you?

Ross I would appreciate it if you could point it elsewhere.

Ronny I'm not gonna shoot you.

Ross Look, I know you don't want to shoot me but accidents can happen, can't they?

Ronny I got it from the warehouse. You know, the place I did. I found it in a drawer.

Ross Why did you vandalize the . . . ?

Ronny I didn't vandalize it.

Ross I'm sorry . . . I meant . . .

Ronny I know what you mean. I wrecked it, like. I wrecked it, 'cos it deserved wreckin'. It was all rubbish, all of it, but it wasn't vandalism. It was justice. You started it, y'know.

Ross Look, man, I don't know what you're talking . . .

Ronny If I hadn't listened to your show. I wouldn't have heard the advert, would I?

Ross Which?

Ronny You know which advert. That *Soundpack*. Music at your fingertips. Be a real musician? It's just a box of tapes, isn't it? Pre-recorded tapes, that's all . . . isn't it? Eh? Eh?

Ross I don't know, man . . .

Ronny Don't "man" me! A four-year-old kid could play one of them. You put it out, don't you, as though all you have to do is buy one of them, an' you'll be a great musician. Lies, you see . . . lies again. You press the keys, an' all it does it set off a load of tapes inside. It's not me who's playin' though, is it? Eh? It's the feller who put the music on the tape in the first place, isn't it? He's doin' the playin' . . . not me.

Ross I'm not responsible for the jingles. You can't blame me for the jingles, man.

Ronny When I smashed up all them *Soundpack* things in that warehouse, I was doin' people a favour—it wasn't vandalism.

But they never listen. Even when you try an' tell people to stop
listenin' to the lies they still go on doin' it. When you tell them
that it's a con, all of it, they don't listen to you. They'll listen
tonight, though. They'll have to, 'cos I'll be shoutin' it out
through every radio in town.

SCENE 10

The police station

Sergeant (*on the telephone*) Yes . . . yeah . . . yes . . . I've heard it,
madam. Yes. Well I . . . yes . . . yes, I . . . er . . . yes. Well, I think
you'll find that it's just a play. A drama. Yes . . . that's right. No
need to worry now. OK. Thank you. (*He puts the telephone
down.*) I don't know. They can't tell fact from fiction out there.

The telephone rings

Not another. Here, you take this one.
Constable (*on the telephone*) Yes . . . hello . . . Well, I think . . . Oh.
Yeah . . . I see . . . could you just hold on a second, please? (*He
turns to the Sergeant*) Sarge, I've got a feller here who says that
the lad in the studio is the one who jumped the van today.
Sergeant Rubbish. He's gettin' the news mixed up with the fiction.
Constable What shall I say?
Sergeant Here . . . give me the phone. (*He takes the phone*) Hello,
sir. Sergeant Morison here . . . yes . . . Well, don't worry, sir . . .
I'm sure you'll find that it's just an invented thing . . . yes . . . yes,
all right . . . OK. Thank you. (*To the Constable*) Switch it on. I
don't know. If they're gonna do realistic plays, you'd think
they'd give some sort of an explanation first.

*The Constable switches on the radio and the voices of Ronny and
Ross are heard through the radio*

Ronny An' how do I work it so that I'm broadcastin'?
Ross I'll switch on for you.
Ronny Right. Go on . . . What's that light goin' on for?
Ross That's a cue light. It means get ready. When the other light
comes on, it means you're live.
Ronny Go on. Switch on.

Ross switches on

OK. Right. This is, er, Ronny Heron here. I've ... er ... I've come to tell you about the lies. You know, the lies that you hear all day on this radio station. See, I found out. Like before, when they was puttin' out the news an' they said that I vandalized that warehouse. Well, that was a lie. You'd think the news would be honest, wouldn't you? But it's not. They said that I vandalized that warehouse. But I didn't. I wrecked it. Oh yeah, smashed everything' up, but it wasn't vandalism. If you bought one of them *Soundpacks* y'd know what I mean.

Constable I'll get the car, Sarge.

Sergeant Just hold on.

Ronny But not only that. Everythin' else is the same. Look, like, you know that advert, the one for the tee shirts, the one where they say all you have to do is get one of these tee shirts, an' then you'll get loads of dates. Well you won't, you know. Wearin' one of them tee shirts won't make any difference at all. People should start to realize that. It's the same with all the stuff they tell you about on this station an' on the telly an' the sides of buses. You know, the stuff that they say'll change your life. Well, listen, it won't. All the tee shirts, an' cars, an' washing machines, an' fridges, an' radios, an' stereos, knife sharpeners, holidays, books, an' make-up, an' things that they sell you— none of it'll ever change you, y'know, if you're no good in the first place. If you're no good, you stay no good. An' the lies that they tell you, the lies about all them things, if you believe them, they just make it worse for you. An' you know what the biggest lie is, eh? You know the biggest lie of all? The music! That's the killer. 'Cos you listen to it, don't you? At night, out there, you listen to the music driftin' out an' it makes you feel good, doesn't it? As though everything's good around you an' inside you. When the music plays, it's as though the world was made for *you*, an', an' tomorrow's gonna be a good day, an' everythin's gonna be all right, an' every road goes somewhere. There's birds singin', an' the moon's always big an' yellow. There's a girl to love you an' hold you an' look after you forever. But it's only music, you know. It's only a load of tapes in a box, really.

Constable Shall I get the car?

Ronny I just wanted to tell you that.

Constable Shall I, Sarge?

Sergeant I dunno, lad.

Constable Well you heard him. It's Heron all right.

Ronny (*to Ross*) Switch that off. Switch it off.

Sergeant How do we know it is Heron? Say it's just a play?

Constable Well, a play wouldn't be about today's news would it?

Sergeant That's the sort of thing they do these days. Documen-
tary sort of things. I mean, what I'm worried about is supposin'
it is just a play. Suppose it is, an' we get a car round there. I can
just see tomorrow's news bulletin: "Police move in to arrest
radio play!" We'd be a laughin' stock.

Constable Sarge, that's not a play. It's happenin' now. It's the
truth.

Sergeant All right, get a car. We'll take a look.

SCENE 11

The radio studio

Ronny You know the worst thing, eh, Ross? Eh? I'll tell you.
When they pick me up for this one, they'll send me for reports.
You know psychiatrists like. Soft, isn't it? They'll treat me as
though I'm mad, because I wanted to tell the truth.

Ross Look, if you split now you could still . . .

Ronny No point. I might as well wait here, an' get a free ride to the
cop shop.

Ross You're just gonna give yourself up, quietly? No shooting?
Look man, it'll do you no good. You start letting that thing off,
man, an' it's gonna be a lot more than Borstal for you.

Ronny Start shootin'! I'd have a job, wouldn't I? It's a toy gun! A
replica! Some people, I dunno, they'd believe anythin'.

Ross You could have told me that before, couldn't you?

Ronny It makes a change though, doesn't it Ross? You bein'
fooled for once, instead of you foolin' everyone else. That's
prime, that is.

Ross Listen, you . . . when the coppers get here, you better tell
them straight off that that gun isn't real.

Ronny Why? What you worried about, Ross?

Ross They might be armed.

Ronny The coppers! Armed? They're comin' to get *me*. Not Al
Capone. You've been watchin' too many films, mate.

Ross Look. You just tell them as soon as they get here. Right?

Ronny Since when have you been givin' orders round here?

Ross Listen idiot. When you thought we weren't on the air, we
were. Right? The police, out there, they'll think you've got a real
gun. Why do you think it's taken so long for them to get here?
They'll have been organizing armed men to come and get you.

Ronny You said it wouldn't be going out. You said that was the
truth. You just can't stop lyin', can you? Why couldn't you just
tell the truth for once?

Ross It's your own fault. You lied to me. You told me that gun
was real.

Ronny I didn't lie. It is real.

Ross Oh, come on. You . . .

Ronny I lied when I told you it was a dummy.

Ross I don't believe you.   .

Ronny Don't you? Right! (*He presses the gun to Ross's head*)

Ross Take that away from my head.

Ronny Shall I pull the trigger?

Ross Look, get that away from my head. Listen, please, please,
man . . .

Ronny I thought you didn't believe me.

Ross I believe you. Please take the gun away.

Ronny You better had believe me, an' all. 'Cos the gun is real. An'
it's loaded. An' I'm not goin' quietly. I'm goin' out of here
shootin'.

Ross Please let me get out first.

Ronny Why? You're my passport, Ross. My passport to freedom.
With you as a hostage, I can get away from here. I can make
them get me a plane.

Ross You're not gonna try that one. Man, you've been listening to
too much news.

Ronny I'm not goin' to Borstal. If they don't get me a plane out of
the country, you're a dead man.

Ross Don't be stupid. That only happens in stories. It's not real.

Ronny We'll see about that.

The Sergeant enters in the next studio

Sergeant Heron!

Ronny Who's that?

Sergeant Heron! This is the police. Look through the glass. I'm in the next studio. Can you see me?

Ronny Yeah. I can see you.

Ross He can't hear you. Press that switch. Talk through that mike.

Sergeant Can you hear me, Heron?

Ronny Yeah. I can hear you . . .

Ross Don't shoot . . . just don't . . .

Ronny Shut it, you . . .

Sergeant Right lad. Put the gun down.

Ronny Get lost.

Sergeant Just put it down, an' no one will get hurt.

Ronny I decide who gets hurt. Listen. Do what I tell you, an' everyone'll be happy. I wanna get out of here right? Now I wanna car to get me an' Ross to the airport, an' I wanna plane waitin' to take . . .

Sergeant Come on, Ronny, lad, you've been listenin' to too many plays. Just come back down to earth, an' everything'll be all right.

Ronny Oh, it'll be great, won't it! Everything'll be wonderful! I'm tellin' you, either I get out of here to a waitin' plane, or I do Ross in.

Ross Please . . . please do as he says . . .

Ronny That's right . . . do as I say, or Ross gets it.

Sergeant I don't believe that you'd do that, Ronny.

Ronny Well, you better had believe me.

Sergeant Come on, Ronny. I'm coming in there now . . .

Ross Don't . . . please . . .

Ronny I'll shoot him . . . I'm tellin' you . . . Don't you try it. Get back! I'm warnin' you . . . get back . . .

The Sergeant and Constable enter the studio

Sergeant Right, Ronny, give me the gun.

Ronny Get out! Get back! I'll put one in you first . . .

Sergeant No you won't! Come on . . . come on . . . now . . .

There is a scuffle

Right . . . hold him, Constable. Good lad, hold him there. You all right sir?

Ross sighs with relief

Who were you gonna shoot with this, Ronny? Mm? You would have been better off with a water pistol. Didn't anyone tell you, Heron, if you're gonna shoot anyone, you have to get a real gun first. Come on, let's be havin' you.

SCENE 12

The radio studio

It is the next day

Newscaster This is Peter French with the mid-day news. Following last night's dramatic scenes here at Radio Ford, a youth, Ronald Arthur Heron, has appeared before a special magistrates' court. Heron, who said nothing during the two minute hearing, was remanded for psychiatric reports. For the full details of last night's drama we go over to the man who was at the centre of the ordeal, Radio Ford's DJ Paul Ross.

Ross Perhaps the most terrifying experience I've ever gone through. The ... er ... the worst thing about it was when, as lots of listeners will have heard, he started ranting on about truth, you know. Er ... I mean, I knew then that I was dealing with someone who was totally unpredictable.

Interviewer You mean you got the impression that he was disturbed?

Ross Yeah. I ... well ... you know, I knew then that I was dealing with a madman.

The sound of John Lennon and the Beatles singing I Read the News Today *fades in and drowns out Ross and the interviewer*

SOUND PLOT